SOCCER
FOR FUN AND FITNESS

Ty Schalter

Enslow Publishing
101 W. 23rd Street
Suite 240
New York, NY 10011
USA
enslow.com

Published in 2020 by Enslow Publishing, LLC.
101 W. 23rd Street, Suite 240, New York, NY 10011

Library of Congress Cataloging-in-Publication Data

Names: Schalter, Ty author.
Title: Soccer for fun and fitness / Ty Schalter.
Description: New York : Enslow Publishing, 2020 | Series: Sports for fun and fitness | Audience: Grade level for this book is K-4. | Includes bibliographical references and index.
Identifiers: LCCN 2019011911| ISBN 9781978513471 (library bound) | ISBN 9781978513457 (paperback) | ISBN 9781978513464 (6 pack)
Subjects: LCSH: Soccer--Juvenile literature.
Classification: LCC GV943.25 .S33 2019 | DDC 796.334--dc23
LC record available at https://lccn.loc.gov/2019011911

Printed in the United States of America

To Our Readers: We have done our best to make sure all website addresses in this book were active and appropriate when we went to press. However, the author and the publisher have no control over and assume no liability for the material available on those websites or on any websites they may link to. Any comments or suggestions can be sent by email to customerservice@enslow.com.

Photo Credits: Soccer – Research by Bruce Donnola

Cover, p. 1 (soccer players) Alistair Berg/DigitalVision/Getty Images; cover and interior pages (balls and birdie) Lightspring/Shutterstock.com; p. 7 pixfly/Shutterstock.com; p. 9 Jam Media/ Getty Images; p. 10 IS2008-12/Alamy Stock Photo; pp. 13, 25 © iStockphoto.com/matimix; p. 15 © iStockphoto.com/AleksandarNakic; p. 16 © iStockphoto.com/pic4you; p. 20 © iStockphoto. com/kali9; p. 21 © iStockphoto.com/Steve Debenport; p. 22 © iStockphoto.com/Serhiy Divin; p. 26 © iStockphoto.com/nycshooter; p. 27 Steve Skjold/Alamy Stock Photo

Contents

Introduction

There's no more fun way to get fit than by playing soccer—and around the world, more people play soccer to have fun and get fit than any other sport! The Fédération Internationale de Football Association (FIFA), who runs the World Cup tournament, estimates that 265 million people play soccer. That's because soccer is for *everyone*.

Whether it's on a school playground or in a huge stadium, all you need to play soccer is a ball and some people who want to play. You don't need a helmet or a bat or special shoes. You can even develop your soccer skills and get active all by yourself.

But you *can* play on a team—and if you want to be the best player you can be, and get in great shape, that's the best choice to make. Competitive soccer players run, walk, and sprint almost nonstop. Professional soccer players cover miles of ground every single game, more than any other athletes.

But it's not just running around! Whether it's using skills and speed to beat opponents one-on-one or team-work and quick passes to create scoring opportunities, great soccer players use their brains to make all that hard work pay off.

Maybe you've watched soccer during the World Cup or the Olympics. Maybe you've seen games on TV or amazing goals online. The colors and flags, smoke bombs and singing, neon **cleats** and wild haircuts are fun to watch, but it's even more fun to get out there and play.

Amazing athletes didn't start playing in fancy uniforms or for cheering fans. They started with a ball and their body, and maybe some friends, and might have used some backpacks for **goal posts**.

Whether you want to be like the pros, represent your school, or just have fun with your friends, you can get started the same way.

C H A P T E R 1

Kickoff!

Soccer is a simple game. It's played on a rectangular field with two goals placed at the opposite long ends. There are two teams and one ball. Each team is trying to put the ball in the other team's goal. The only catch is that you can't catch it—it's against the rules to touch the ball with your arms or hands!

Soccer players kick the ball to move it forward, pass to their teammates, and score goals in the opponent's net. When the clock reaches **full time**, the team with the most goals wins.

Every game starts the same: two players in the center
of the field with the ball, ready to kick off!

First Kick

Soccer can be played with any number of players—even
just one on each team! The fewer players there are, and
the younger they are, the smaller the field should be.
Try to set up the goals so that nobody playing can kick

THE WORLD'S GAME

The World Cup Finals, held every four years, determines which country has the world's best national soccer team. Most countries have professional leagues, like Major League Soccer in the United States. Those teams compete every year in their home leagues, as well as in tournaments like the European Champions League.

the ball all the way from one goal to the other, but not much farther than that.

When you're playing with a few players per team, don't worry much about specific positions. Even pros work on their skills by practicing in small teams on small fields, running and attacking and defending all as a group.

Getting in Position

There are three main position groups: forwards, midfielders, and defenders. Forwards mostly play offense and try to score goals. Defenders mostly play defense, working with the goalie to keep the ball out of their own net. Midfielders need to be strong runners as they join forwards in attack and defenders in defense and try to move the ball from their own end of the field to their opponent's end.

Wait, what was that bit about a "goalie"?

The World Cup is an international tournament for soccer teams. Thirty-two teams go to the World Cup every year.

Goalies try to prevent the other team from scoring goals. They are the only players who can regularly use their hands.

One player on each team is named the goalkeeper. That player stays in front of their team's goal. Goalkeepers are the only players who can use their hands to stop opponents' shots. They can pick up the ball to throw or punt it to a teammate.

Some people call them goalies, and others call them keepers. They're a very important part of a team's defense and help to get the ball rolling on offense. Playing goalie can be boring when the ball is on the other side of the field, and it can be frustrating when you let in a goal.

If you like playing goalie, it's important not to play that position all the time. You won't develop the kicking and passing skills you need to get better, and you won't run nearly as much as all the other players—so you won't get as fit, either.

If you don't like playing goalie, it's important to try it sometimes anyway. Understanding how a goalie works with their defenders, how a goalie passes upfield, and how a goalie moves to stop shots will make you a better player overall.

CHAPTER 2

· ·

Solo Skills

Your feet are at the heart of soccer. If you can't keep the ball with you when you run, pass accurately to a teammate, accept a pass from a teammate, or shoot on goal, you won't be very useful on a soccer field—and you won't get any exercise, either.

The good news is that all you need to build up your ball skills are your feet and a ball!

Be the Ball

Without shoes, set one foot on the ball and try to roll the ball in a small circle using only that foot. Roll it straight

Since you can't use your hands, learning to use your feet is vital for soccer! Special shoes called cleats can help.

out front as far as you can, and pull it back underneath you without letting go. Do the same thing to the side and to the back.

Then build it up: switch feet, roll the ball in bigger circles, roll it faster, keep your balance better. Try figure-eights. Make up new movements. Try it in shoes and in cleats. A few minutes a day can help you get better!

Dribbling in soccer is much like basketball, only with feet and not hands. The faster you can run while dribbling, the harder you'll be to stop. Practice going slowly, with small touches on the ball, then building speed without losing control. Think of keeping the ball "on a string," as if it were a yo-yo on your foot. Alternate your left and right foot, and try going around cones.

Juggling, or keepy uppie, is great practice for your **first touch**. Try to kick the ball up as many times in a row as you can without letting it hit the ground. The key is very soft, quick kicks. Hint: Practice standing still on one leg to improve your balance!

Kicking with Accuracy

Accuracy is important, and the instep strike is usually the right choice. Imagine a smiley face on the ball: two eyes up top, a smile along the bottom, and a nose in the middle. For an instep strike, you want to bop the ball right on its nose with the curved inside part of your foot.

To practice, set your ball a few feet from a wall you have permission to kick it against. Plant one foot along-side the ball and "bop its nose" with the inside of the other foot. If you do it right, the ball will hit the wall

Juggling is a fun soccer skill, where you try to keep the ball from touching the ground, using only your feet.

Freestyle soccer lets you show off fancy kicks and tricks, often using moves from gymnastics.

and come straight back. Practice with both feet, moving farther away from the wall, and seeing how many times in a row you can kick it without having to move.

Kicking with Power

To take a hard shot on goal, you want to put your laces on the ball. Kick the ball and hit the nose of the ball with the *top* of your foot. Imagine driving your shoelaces through the ball. It takes practice, but you can kick the ball much harder this way.

FREESTYLE!

Freestyle soccer blends extreme technical skill with fitness, balance, flexibility, and agility. One person uses a soccer ball to show off flashy kicks and tricks, control elements, and even gymnastic moves and athleticism. Freestyle is as hard as it is awesome.

Learning some freestyle basics will challenge you as an athlete, improve your ball control, and give you the chance to impress your friends—all without leaving your yard!

17

To hit the ball far, like for a **corner kick**, **goal kick**, or long pass, start from a few steps back. Jog up to the ball, plant your foot a little farther to the side than usual, straighten out your kicking leg, and try to hit the ball's "smile" with the area where your foot meets your ankle. Think of swinging your leg like a baseball bat. When you get it right, your foot will naturally wrap around the ball as you launch it into the air.

CHAPTER 3

Being Part of a Team

No matter how good you get at kicking a ball against a wall or dribbling around cones, you won't be able to reach your physical peak unless you're challenging yourself against competition.

Why Compete?

Competition is fun. Passing to teammates, scoring a goal, or making a great **tackle** can't be done by yourself.

Soccer is a team sport, and it's important to listen to your coach in order to play your best.

You also can't push yourself to be the best you can be without competition. You might think you can run fast, but you'll never know how fast until you have to beat a defender to score a goal—or catch an opponent from behind while they're about to take a shot.

When You Don't Have the Ball

Always be aware of your teammates, your opponents, and where you should be in relation to them. Good teams work together on both sides of the ball.

Depending on what position you play, you often won't be the one with **possession** of the ball. Try to stay in the area your coach assigns you. If you're a defender, don't run in front of the forwards or block your own goalie.

If you are on defense or offense, you'll play your best by working with your teammates.

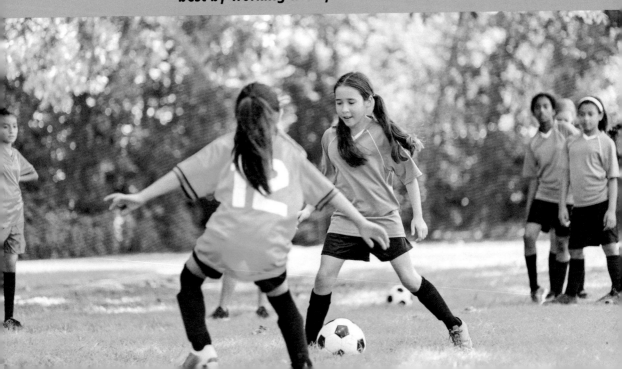

When you get the ball, remember all you've learned and that you aren't alone on the field. You're working as part of a team to play your best game.

If you aren't sure what to do, talk to your teammates! Learn your teammates' names, and use them on the field. Your coach may teach you other words to use that will help you communicate with your teammates, like saying "square" to mean you're open for a sideways pass.

No matter what, always be thinking about what's going to happen next.

FINDING A TEAM

There are lots of ways to play. You can join pickup games at school recess or after school. Check out your local parks and recreation department for beginner youth leagues. There are also dedicated soccer facilities, indoor and outdoor, that almost always have their own teams or leagues. Junior highs and high schools also usually have their own teams.

When You've Got the Ball

It's finally happened: You're on a team, and your teammate passed the ball to you! Opponents are running at you to try to take it away—what next?

First, relax.

Nobody makes their best decisions when panicking, and it's hard to use proper technique when you're rushing or tense. Look for your teammates and for open space. Is a teammate calling for a pass? Has the goalie left a spot open by the near post? Now's the time when all your practicing and training pays off!

CHAPTER 4

Safety First
and Last

Practicing the techniques you've learned in this book and from your coach will help you perform skills without looking down or thinking about it, freeing your eyes and brain to work at their peak. But what about your body? You can't play well if you aren't fit, and you can't play at all if you're injured.

Gear

Soccer doesn't require lots of pads like football does, but you do need shin guards. Properly fitting shin guards are a requirement to play in most leagues. They'll protect your lower legs from both the ball and other players. Special shoes called cleats will help you run faster and strike the ball more consistently than regular sneakers

Shin guards will keep your legs safe from the ball and from accidental kicks from other players.

Soccer involves a lot of running, and to run your best, you should stay hydrated at all times.

will. Helmets aren't required, but if you bump your head, be sure to get checked out by your coach.

Hydration

Soccer players run more than athletes in any other sport. It has been estimated that a professional soccer player runs 9.5 miles (15.28 km) over the course of a game. All that running means you need to replace the water your body loses in sweat. Be sure to keep a water bottle on the sidelines so you can stay hydrated!

Fair Play

Remember that everyone on the field came to play and have fun like you did. It's easy to get upset when a play doesn't go your way, but good sportsmanship on the field

The other team is just like your team—they want to have fun and play their best. Thank them for a good game!

NOT ALLOWED

You don't get to use your hands in soccer (unless you're the goalie or tossing a ball back into play), but what else should you avoid? In most youth leagues, and almost all practices, diving and sliding is not allowed. This is to protect you and other players from injury. Older players can also use their heads to strike the ball, but US Soccer forbids kids under thirteen from doing that.

is just as important as mastering skills. **Officials** are there to help you learn the rules, so don't argue with them if they make a call against you. If you have a question, ask! If a teammate makes a mistake, don't get mad—support them. Respect your fellow players and help them play their best game, so you can play your best game.

Remember, no matter what the score is at the end, every time you play soccer, *you win*—because you got a little better, got a little fitter, and had a lot of fun!

Words to Know

cleats Special shoes worn only on grass, with hard rubber nubs on the bottom for traction.

corner kick A free kick from the nearest corner of the field.

dribbling Running with control of the ball.

first touch How well a player tends to control the ball when their feet first touch it.

full time When the clock has reached the total number of minutes the match is supposed to take.

goal kick When a player kicks the ball out of bounds over their opponent's goal line (often because they missed a shot toward goal), the other team's goalie gets a free kick to get the ball going the other way.

goal posts The two vertical posts of a soccer goal.

officials Specially trained people in charge of enforcing the rules in sports.

possession Control of the ball.

tackle Taking the ball from someone.

Learn More

Books

Folger, Carlos, and Deborah W. Crisfield. *The Everything Kids' Soccer Book.* New York, NY: Simon & Schuster, 2018.

Gifford, Clive. *Soccer: Personal Best.* New York, NY: Rosen Publishing, 2018.

Hornby, Hugh. *Eyewitness Soccer.* New York, NY: DK Publishing, 2018.

Websites

Active Kids

activekids.com/soccer

This site includes drills and skill-building activities, as well as tools to search for teams, leagues, camps, and competitions near you.

US Soccer

ussoccer.com

The US Soccer federation oversees youth development, coaching, and competitions in America, and it also develops and runs the youth and adult national competitive teams.

World Freestyle Football Association

thewffa.org

This is the official site of the world governing body of freestyle soccer. Check out rules, getting-started resources, and videos.

Index

D
dribbling, 14, 19

E
European Champions League, 8

F
Fédération Internationale de
    Football Association (FIFA), 4
field, 6, 7, 9, 11, 12, 22, 27
first touch, 14
freestyle soccer, 17

G
gear, 25
    cleats, 5, 14, 25
    shin pads, 25

I
instep strike, 14

K
kicks, 14, 17
    corner kick, 18
    goal kick, 18

L
leagues, 8, 25, 28
    beginner youth, 23

Major League Soccer, 8
soccer facilities, 23

O
officials, 28
Olympics, 5

P
positions, 8, 11, 21
    defenders, 8, 9, 11, 19, 20, 21
    forwards, 8, 9, 21
    goalie (goalkeeper), 8, 9, 11, 21,
        23, 28
    midfielders, 8, 9

R
rules, 6, 28

S
skills, 4, 5, 8, 11, 12, 17, 24, 28
sportsmanship, 27

T
tackle, 19
teams, 4, 6

W
World Cup, 4, 5, 8